MAY   '76

APR   1992

JUL   '66

APR

KVCC   LIBRARY   COLLEGE

28148

The
Poet and Other
Poems

By
Raymond Garfield Dandridge

Cincinnati, Ohio
1920

Library of Congress Cataloging in Publication Data

Dandridge, Raymond Garfield.
   The poet and other poems.

   Reprint of the 1920 ed. published by Powell & White,
Cincinnati.
   I. Title.
PS3507.A567P6   1975   811'.5'4   73-18573
ISBN 0-404-11384-2

Reprinted from the edition of 1920, Cincinnati
First AMS edition published in 1975
Manufactured in the United States of America

AMS PRESS INC.
NEW YORK, N. Y. 10003

IN MEMORY OF
MY BROTHER

Oscar William Dandridge

Contents

FOREWORD

T is a pleasure and an honor for me to write a brief foreword concerning the remarkable genius of the author of this sunny medley of poems.

Even the most casual perusal of these pages will impress the reader with the wide range of thought displayed by the author. Only an inkling, however, is given of his unconquerable spirit. Shut in within four walls by a strange decree of nature for many long years, racked at times by the most excruciating pains, denied free intercourse among his fellow-men and handicapped in a thousand other ways, he has overcome all these and composed these spritely lines.

This book and an earlier one should serve as a ray of light to those whose activity is curtailed by nature. They prove that although a man may become helpless from his shoulders down, he may exceed the wildest dreams of his friends if he has the perseverance and application to develop his latent talents from the shoulders up.

The winning fight of Mr. Ray G. Dandridge, in producing a work of art in the midst of a constant battle with nature, has won for him a prominent place among the poets of the Ohio valley and a commanding position among the literary minded of his race.

Born and reared on Price Hill, educated at the Whittier School, Mr. Dandridge is a true product of Cincinnati. His poems are based for the most part on his reflections on the earlier, active part of his life but he has, nevertheless, remained alive to the poetic possibilities of current events.

His poems, "Roosevelt," in which he utilizes the last words of the late ex-President, and "The Heritage" show his deep interest in the affairs of today. His dialect poems are particularly striking and true to life. His poems, "The Poet," quaint, homely but too often true, "To an Unhanged Judas," "Zalka Peetruza," "Red Rose," "Old Glory," "Ease," and "Toil Created" portray a wonderful insight and appreciation of things worth while outside of the intrinsic value of the verse.

The fame of the author has exceeded the limits of his boyhood suburb and his new book will no doubt add many new friends and admirers. I can only say in conclusion that he has my sincerest best wishes for continued success and that the last stanza of his poem "The Poet" will not hold good in his case:

"Who mock his song, deny him bread,
Then sing his praise when he is dead."

WINSTON V. MORROW.

The Poet and Other Poems

THE POET

The poet sits and dreams and dreams;
He scans his verse; he probes his themes.

Then turns to stretch or stir about,
Lest, like his thoughts, his strength give out.

Then off to bed, for he must rise
And cord some wood, or tamp some ties,

Or break a field of fertile soil,
Or do some other manual toil.

He dare not live by wage of pen,
Most poorly paid of poor paid men,

With shoes o'er-run, and thread bare clothes,
And editors among the foes

Who mock his song, deny him bread,
Then sing his praise when he is dead.

TIME TO DIE

Black Brother, think you life so sweet
That you would live at any price?
Does mere existence balance with
The weight of your great sacrifice?
Or, can it be you fear the grave
Enough to live and die a slave?
O, Brother! be it better said,
When you are gone and tears are shed,
That your death was the stepping stone
Your children's children cross'd upon.
Men have died that men might live:
Look every foeman in the eye!
If necessary, your life give
For something, ere in vain you die.

OLD GLORY

God's placid heavens mother you,
His sunsets blend your bars,
His endless fields of midnight blue
Serve background for your stars.

So near immortal Emblem grand,
Cradled in the sky,
As long as earth and heavens stand,
You will not—shall not die!

A RECALLED PRAYER

Sis Hannah May Liza, so Emphraim
    sayed,
Stole out 'neaf a sycamo' tree an'
    prayed
To de Lawd in Hebbin, an' she ast
    dat He
W'u'd please sen' her a man
    fo' company.

Her prayah wuz answered; fo' a
    week wen' 'roun',
De Arch Decon Mordecai Joshua
    Brown
Ast Sis Hannah w'u'den she
    share his lot,
His hoss an' his buggy, his boa'd
    an' his cot.

Straight away she etcepted,
    an' soon dey wor wed,
"Fo' bettah or wussah" de
    preachah man sed;
An' Hannah wuz happy, she thot
    dat she knowed
She had a reel he'p-mate to
    he'p tote de load.

De honeymoon riz, den it sot in
        its tracks,
W'en Hannah, po' Hannah, 'gan
        gazin on facks.
De bank book he flourished
        wuz long ovahdrawn,
An' paymint wuz jue on de
        close he had on.

De hoss an' de buggy, he ast her
        to share,
Belonged to his boss-man
        (Jedge Hinton Sinclair).
His boa'd an' his cot she foun'
        meagah an' slim,
In fack, his 'hole lot wuzen
        nuthin' 'cept him.

Den Probitshun cut Jedge's
        dockit so low
He foun' hisse'f forced to let
        Mordecai go;
An' seemed dar wuz nary one else roun'
        de town
Dat had wuk quite suited to
        Mordecai Brown.

Meanw'ile, Hannah labahed,
    bofe early an' late,
W'ile Mordecai armed wid
    pipe, pole an' bait,
Sot down by de ribbah,
    or loafed in de shade,
Or stood lookin' on w'ile
    de checkahs wuz played.

Et Barbah Shop sessions he'd
    freely discuss
Shakespeare, League ob Nations,
    Stock Markit an' Truss;
Et Church or Class Meetin',
    comman' in' de flo',
He'd tell ob God's Glory whar
    man's wuk is o'.

His appetite waxed, an' his
    drowsiness grew,
'Till eatin' an' sleepin' wuz
    all he w'u'd do.
Bofe meal time an' bed time
    he met wid a vim,
But all uddah labahs proved
    strangahs to him.

Enste'd ob he'p light'nin' po'
    Sis Hannah's load,
De Decon klum up on her burden
    an' rode.
Once mo', she stole out, 'neaf
    de varie same tree,
An' prayed, "Lawd, please
    Lawdy! taik dat man frum me."

RED ROSE

I plucked a rose, a red rose rare,
I placed her on a throne
Within my heart; and there I dare
To worship her alone.

An idol, thus, I paid to her
My constant vigil, love, and care.
Upon my knees, I prayed to her,
My whole heart in my prayer.

Alas! my love, my care, my prayer,
Failed! failed to keep my treasure fair.
I saw (my heart filled with despair)
    Her drooping head;

Her beauty, grace and fragrance flown,
Her every leaf and petal shorn,
I gazed in silence—and alone—
    Upon my dead.

A RESOLUTION

Mah ruddah's brokin, an' mah sail
Wen' ovah bode, in las' night's gale;
Mah bunkah's empty, steam am low,
Ise driftin' wid de undah tow.

Mah neighbah's bark goes skippin' by,
Wid breeze fat sail, 'neaf clear blue sky;
Seems lak de bes' ob bes' am his,
W'ile mine is all de wust whut is.

But mebbe sumthin', I cain't see,
Maiks mah neighbah envy me:
Purhaps I w'u'd hab differn views
Ef I wuz stan'in' in his shoes.

So, 'ste'd ob grumblin' 'bout mah lot,
I'll do mah bes' wid whut I got;
Kaze He doan ast dat eny man
Do bettah dan de bes' he can.

SONGS AND SMILES

Well-meaning friends often ask,
Am I not weary of my task,
And how I dare give voice to song—
I who have lain thus so long.

Many the times a quizzing thought
Has asked of me why I have sought
To sing my songs, though oft in pain,
And if my songs are not in vain.

To quizzing thought and you, dear friends,
I fear I offer no amends,
Except that I find songs and smiles
Help lessen intervening miles
'Twixt me and yonder peaceful crest,
Where I shall rest.

TRUE FREN

You sez dat ole frens am de best.
I begs yore pawden, deed I do,
Kaze I think he is mighty blest
Who hab a true fren, ole or new.

TO AN UNHANGED JUDAS

Cannibalistic vulture,
Grown fat upon your brother's blood,
The Tide you do not seek to stem
Engulfs you in its flood.

The cords you bind about his hands,
Hold your hands doubly fast;
And when you rend his anchor chain,
Your bark adrift you cast.

The day you snuff his light of hope,
And dim ambition's guiding spark,
You doom yourself to ever grope
In tractless waste of endless dark.

O! blasphemer of sacred trust,
Go hide your dirty, double face!
Far better were you dead at birth
Than live to sacrifice your Race.

Vile cringing cur, unfit to hang,
Live long to writhe in pain
Beneath on-marching feet of those
Who fall—to rise again.

VALUATION

No man can shape his destiny,
Though ardent his desire,
Or shift his heavy load elsewhere,
Should he perchance to tire.
Though weak or mighty he may be,
Though he may "choose and fend,"
The given road allotted him
Is his road to the end.

The plodding soul was born to plod,
The foiler born to foil;
The driver born to wield the rod,
The toiler born to toil.
'Tis not the prestige of your cast
Among the roles of earth,
But how well you do what you do
That demonstrates your worth.

RETRIBUTION

Rent and bleeding,
Upon her knees
She cried, "Mercy!"
The voice of Justice,
Mockingly, inquired,
"What of mercy have you shown?"
Four hundred thousand,
Armless colonists,
Raised nubs—grim evidence.

'ITTLE TOUZLE HEAD

(To R. V. P.)

Cum, listen w'ile yore Unkel sings,
  Erbout how low sweet chariot swings,
Truint Angel, wifout wings,
  Mah 'ittle Touzle Head.

Stop! Stop! how dare you laff et me,
  Bekaze I foul de time an' key,
Thinks you dat I is Black Pattie,
  Mah 'ittle Touzle Head?

O, Honey Lam'! dem sparklin' eyes,
  Dat offen laffs an' selem cries,
Is sho a God gib natchel prize,
  Mah 'ittle Touzle Head.

An' doze wee han's so sof' an' sweet,
  Mates wid dem toddlin', velvet feet,
Jes to roun' you out, complete,
  Mah 'ittle Touzle Head.

Sma't! youse sma't ez sma't kin be,
  Knows yore evah A, B, C,
Plum on down to X, Y, Z,
  Mah 'ittle Touzle Head.

De man doan know how much he miss,
  Ef he ain't got no neice lak dis;
Fro yore Unkel one mo' kiss,
  Mah 'ittle Touzle Head!

I wist sum magic w'u'd ellow,
  (By charm or craf'—doan mattah how)
You stay jes lak you is right now,
  Mah 'ittle Touzle Head.

MEMORIES

I am as fond of fun and jokes
As other real red-blooded folks.

I relish bits of breezy spice,
Within the bounds considered "nice;"

And do not think, because I'm down,
That I must whine and wear a frown.

I love to eat. I love to drink.
I love to be alone and think

Of faded days, and of the girls
Whose mem'ries are a string of pearls.

No matter what the bliss to-day,
To-morrow finds it in decay,

And likewise every sorrow flees,
Leaving only memories.

TO A BIRD

Sweet singer, how I envy you,
Faint, fleeting, speck 'gainst azure hue.
You have gone up to chant your lay,
While I must be content to stay
Below, and gaze, with hungry eyes,
Upon you, soaring t'ward the prize.

ROOSEVELT.

"Put out the light!"
He had no need of man-made glow
With celestial Dawn in sight:
Unflinchingly, we saw him go
Onward, to mount the highest Height.
"Put out the light!"

"Put out the light!"
His noble soul, stranger to fear,
Sought not the guidance of a spark:
His active conscience, ever clear,
Knew little gloom and less of dark.
"Put out the light!"

"Put out the light!"
Apostle of "Preparedness,"
Who lived and died prepared,
Had he not seen a just redress,
Could he—would he have dared
"Put out the light?"

"Put out the light!"
A sacred wreath we hang on high
Upon immortal mem'ry's wall,
To never wither, droop or die,
Until we, too, have heard the call—
"Put out the light!"

SPRIN' FEVAH

Dar's a lazy, sortah hazy
    Feelin' grips me, thoo an' thoo;
An' I feels lak doin' less dan enythin';
    Dough de saw is sharp an' greasy,
Dough de task et han' is easy,
    An' de day am fair an' breezy,
Dar's a thief dat steals embition in de win'.

Kaint defy it, kaint deny it,
    Kaze it jes wont be denied;
Its a mos' pursistin' stubbern sortah thin';
    Anti Tox' doan neutrolize it;
Doctahs fail to analyze it;
    So I yiel's (dough I despise it)
To dat res'less, wretchit fevah
    evah Sprin'.

DAYS

Do tell me, where is yesterday?
All-knowing Sage, I dare thee say
Other than it has been cast
Into the maelstrom of the past.

And tell me of to-morrow, Sage,
If thou canst read an unturn'd page,
And, also, something of to-day
That was to-morrow, yesterday.

DECREED

(Matthew—2:15)

Indirectly, out of Africa you came
By His decree; 'twas no miscarried chance
That bade you face despoilers of His name,
Upon the red-run battle fields of France.

Just so, each word, each jot, and every tittle
That He has ever promised or decreed,
No matter how majestic or how little,
Shall follow in the foot steps of His lead.

A BROOK

Reflecting ragged
Flecks of white,
Upon a background blue,
A living, liquid, ribbon
Slips, zig-zag,
Through meadow land.

Creeping, leaping,
Sighing, singing,
Piu Piano
At even flow,
Crescendo!
At the rapids.

TOIL CREATED

Dutiful, underpaid bearer of burden
(Although as oxen your past roles were cast,
And dark the stage whereon your scene was set)
The wearing of the yoke of toil has been **your**
   alchemist.

Heights imperceptible, by sheer strength surmounted,
Dire circumstance and hind'ring bars o'ercome,
With sinew taut and stamina unyielding,
Complete, you stand a toil created man.

TO——

Though many are the dreams I dream,
They're born within a single theme.
The same kind voice I ever hear,
Instilling faith, upbraiding fear:
The same consoling smile appears
To snuff my sighs and dry my tears:
And fondest heart, of purest gold,
Is hers whose name I here withold,
And pray naught ever change my theme,
Or wake me from my dream.

SUPPLICATION

(Dedicated to Cincinnati Branch, N.' A. A. C. P., and
sung to the air, "America")

Dear Lord we come to Thee,
In quest of Liberty,
Thy mercy lend.
We know no better way
Than serve, obey and pray,
Protect us night and day,
Almighty Friend.

Unsheathe Thy vengeful sword,
Cleave us a way, O Lord,
As naught else can.
Let no base foe oppress,
Let no vain thought repress
Our future usefulness
To God and Man.

We have no ancient creed,
We have no glutton's greed
To satisfy.
We seek the lofty height,
Where Justice, Truth and Right,
Condemn oppressor's might,
Like God on High.

May World Democracy
Include equality
For every one.
Father, all-wise and just,
Do as Thou wilt with us,
In Thee, alone, we trust,
"Thy will be done."

FRENSHIP

(To G. B. P.)

I have filched a mite ob time
Fo' de writin' ob dis rhyme.
Seems I c'u'den do a thin'
    ontwil I'd writ it.
Evah man ain' got a fren'
Dat kin stir his lyrick pen,
An' ain' evah one kin feel
Han' clasp lak de grip ob steel:
Consequently, dey dat kin kin
    not fo'git it.

Dat prestige ain' ha'f bad a bit,
An' gole is precious, I'll etmit;
But dar's sumpin' in dis worl' a 'hole
    heap dearah.
It's de knowin' ob a fren'
Dat is yore fren to de en',
Dough de en' en's in a cloud,
Or in a caskit, grave an' shroud,
Yore fren's frenship maiks de
    gloomy outlook clearah.

OPPORTUNITY

The shackles rend, your hands are free,
You need no longer humb'ly bow
Beneath the lash of tyranny;
Go shape the molten metal now.

Behold! "The Door of Hope," ajar,
And Freedom freely beckoning;
She bids you gaze upon a star,
And veer not from your reckoning!

ZALKA PEETRUZA

(Who was christened Lucy Jane)

She danced, near nude, to tom-tom beat,
With swaying arms and flying feet,
'Mid swirling spangles, gauze and lace,
Her all was dancing—save her face.

A conscience, dumb to brooding fears,
Companioned hearing deaf to cheers;
A body, marshalled by the will,
Kept dancing while a heart stood still:

And eyes obsessed with vacant stare
Looked over heads to empty air,
As though they sought to find therein
Redemption for a maiden sin.

'Twas thus, amid force driven grace,
We found the lost look on her face;
And then, to us, did it occur
That, though we saw—we saw not her.

WEDDAH

It wuz cole, de snow dun drifted
Hi' roun' 'bout de ole barn do';
Dun blew thoo de cracks an' sifted
Lines ob white erpon de flo.'
An' de pines wuz bent an' groanin',
Lak dey c'u'den bear no mo';
An' de moanful win' wuz moanin',
Ez it nebbah moaned befo'.

On de ribbah, ice had frozen
Plum ercrost frum sho' to sho';
Jes ez if de Lawd had chosen
Dat it shoulden' run no mo'.
All de folks wuz tired an' weary,
Tired ob ice an' tired ob snow,
Tired ob seein' grey skies, dreary,
An' de murkahree belo'.

W'en et las', dat wretchit weddah
Friz its cruel se'f to deth,
Birds an' trees an' flowers, togeddah,
Bade us draw a natchel bref.
Bade us stroll off in de moonlight,
Wid May Jane or Emmie Lou,
On a pleasen' bawmy June night,
Lak we all wuz wont to do.

Twuzen' long 'fo' dat fair June day
Turnt to Summah's sicknin' heat;
Wid de bode walks, long 'bout noon-day,
Hot ernuff to cook yore feet.
An' you'd meet sum one or uddah,
Drippin', wringin' wet wid sweat,
Or else, heah ob sum po' bruddah
Fallin' out or obah het.

Seems de weddah nebbah pleases,
W'en we hab it boilin' hot
We cry fo' de kine dat freezes,
Alwuz wantin' whut is not.
But it's cleah beyon' our fixin',
Bofe hab faults an' merits, too,
An' de Seasons dats betwixin'
Duzen las' de 'hole yeah thoo.

EASE

Oh! foolish one in quest of ease,
Do you not know that ease on earth, for men,
Is like unto the "Pot of Gold"
        upon the rainbow's end;
A wily "will-o'-the-wisp" who
        flees, and flees, and flees,
Not huriedly, but just a step
        beyond your grasp—is ease?

BROTHER MINE

Prejudice with venom smote
    every word and act;
Snuffed was the light of knowledge
    from your view.
Unbefriended martyr, sole object
    of attack,
Has your fair brother fairly dealt
    with you,
        Brother mine?

Upon defenseless womanhood
    he preyed;
Then freely chatteled blood
    one half his own.
Just punishment has only
    been delayed;
'Tis written; "Ye shall reap
    as ye have sown,"
        Brother mine.

In doctored balance Justice
    balanced you;
In your defense her vengeful
    sword ne'er stirred;
Courts of Law, barring facts,
    basing guilt on hue,
Condemned you, ere the evidence
    was heard—
        Brother mine.

Your constant prayer that you
    might prove your worth
For equal right to struggle,
    live, and die,
So long unheard, unheeded,
    here on earth,
Found audience in One beyond
    the sky—
        Brother mine.

"Vengence is Mine, I will repay!"
    so saith the Lord.
Thusly assured, rail not at
    destiny.
To righteousness He promised
    just reward;
And to the bondman promised
    Liberty—
        Brother mine.

A. L. IMES

Some men go beyond their way
To advertise, in bold display,
The knowledge of the favors they may lend.
Yet, I find one who, if he might,
Would do his best deeds in the night,
And in the darkness bid the matter end.

CENSORED

My Harvah rit me week fo' las',
Dat is, dat's w'en I got it;
He sed, he hardly had de time
'Tween shot an' shell to jot it;
An' dat he had a rail bad cole,
But it wuz gettin' bettah.
Shucks! I disremembah ha'f he rit,
So I'll jes' read his lettah.

"Deah Darlin' Mine: I think ob you
W'ile heah in——" dar it's blotted out.
But dat it twuz sumphin' rail sweet
An' lubin', dar's no doubt.
Den takin' up whar blottin' stop:
"I thanks you fo' de candy,
De sweatah an' de backah, too,
Dey sho wuz fine an' dandy.

"I 'spect to see you, Deah, fo' long,
De Capin sed——" ain't dat a doun right sin,
Jes et de inderestin' part,
Dat blottin' starts ergin?
Aldough I frets, I obahlooks
Caze jes' ez lak ez not,
Dem bullits' whizzin' right an' lef'
Maik enybody blot.

COLOR BLIND

True I am black not by my will;
I had no choice of hue,
And none was given you.
By His decree our roles we fill.
Red man, Yellow man, Brown man,
You too, man of white,
What cause or right
Have we to emphasize our clan?
The haughty King, of royal birth,
The peasant, craftsman, and the slave,
Stript naked, stand alone on worth,
Beyond the portals of the grave,
Before that Bar where all men find
The Judge of judges color blind.

ARISE

Arise! ye humble undertrodden wight,
Behold, at edge of yonder east,
The blazing Sun of Hope adawn!
Think ye not thou needst ever be
The hireling, or an o'er lord's slave;
For He who makes all men, also made thee,
Of sinew, brain, and bone,
And bade thee cleave a bit of earth
Whereon to stand alone.

BETWEEN LINES

(In a little book P. P.)

Learned Sages,
Scan these pages,
Recognize the wealth they hold!
All those places,
That seems spaces,
Golden memories unfold.

Bord'ring edges
Are the ledges,
Whereon rest my rod and staff;
And there's treasure
Beyond measure,
On the fly leaves, fore and aft.

DECEIT

No venomous cobra's stab e'er stung,
Like nectared lies on a false friend's tongue.

Better by far the deadliest foe
Who does not fail to let you know

He is your foe, nor does it smart
As badly, when he rends your heart.

DE INNAH PART

I 'fess Ise ugly, big, an' ruff,
Mah voice is husky, mannah's gruff;
But, mah gal sed, "Neb mine yore hide,
I jedge you by yore inside side;"
An' sed, dat she hab alwuz foun'
De gole beneaf de surfuss groun'.

She claims dat offen rail ruff hides
Am boun' erroun' hi' grade insides;
W'ile sum dat 'pear "sharp ez a tack"
Kinceals a heart dat's hard an' black;
An', to prove her way ob thinkin',
Gibs fo' zample Abeham Linkin.

Ole "Hones' Abe," so lank an' tall,
Worn't no parlah posin' doll:
Yet he stood out miles erbove
Uddah men, in truf an' love.
An' in han'lin' 'fairs of state,
Proved de greates' ob de great.

In makin' great men, Nature mus'
Fo'got erbout de beauty dus',
An' fashun dem frum nachel clay,
De gritty kine, dat doan decay.
But, mos' her time she spent, I know,
Erpon de parts dat duzen show.

AT THE BIER OF HOPE

The night winds drone, in mournful lay,
A solemn requiem o'er the dead.
Lamented Hope of yesterday,
Was there naught you could will instead—
Naught, save a vast uncharted sea
Beset with shoals of misery?
In my heart's blood I dip my pen,
The tears, fast falling, dim my eyes,
A sigh escapes my lips, and then
I strive to rend the binding ties
That stay my hand lest I should write
And, thereby, ease a storm swept mind.
Alas! though I exert my might,
Expressiveness I fail to find.

LOVE

Invisible, saccharined,
  Intoxicating stimulant,
I drank of you—drank deep of you—
  Until drunk, yea! until
Drunk, drunk indeed.

On sobering I find myself
  Unlike the drunkard, blest,
Who sobers with an aching head;
  For I have sobered
With an aching heart.

HAHD CIDAH

Wondah whut on earf tiz ails me,
Seems I see mo' outlan'ish t'ings,
Sech ez wagons pullin' hosses,
An' red mens, wid horns an' wings.
Mussy! how dese steps do tremble,
Dey's jes ez loose ez dey kin be,
An' dat do'-knob thinks it's clevah
Playin' "hide an' seek" wid me.

Dar's a dashah in mah stumick,
Churnin', flip! flop! up an' down:
Mah po' achin' head am spinnin',
Whoop-pee-la-la! roun' an' roun'.
Tongue dun swole up thick ez two tongues:
Goo' Lawd! whut is I to do?
'Speck Ise got de eppazutic,
Or dat ah new fangled "Flu."

I is sartin tizent "Goofoo,"
Caze I ain' ett no strangah's grub,
An' Ise bin nowhar, 'cept callin'
On mah hi brown Lady Lub.
We set coatin', me an' Idah,
'Neaf de arbah, in her yahd,
Holdin' han's an' sippin' cidah
Frum a brown jug, labeled "Hahd."

JUDGE YE NOT

Remember, friend,
  Each harsh word spoken
May descend
  On poor, heart-broken
Wretch, whose road
  Would be the brighter,
If his heavy load
  Were lighter.

Perhaps you,
  Upon the morrow,
May be smitten through
  By sorrow;
Perhaps word
  That you now utter,
Echo heard,
  Would cause a shudder.

"Judge ye not"
  Weak fellow mortal,
Whose dire lot
  And open portal
May admit you
  (In a measure)
To a view
  Bereft of pleasure.

IN FLANDERS FIELDS

(Written after reading "The Appeal," by Lieut. Col. John McCrea; "The Promise," by G. B. Galbreath, and "The Fulfillment," by Joseph A. Clark.)

THE HERITAGE

Row on row the crosses stand;
The breeze blown poppies nod
Approval of the gallant band
Asleep beneath the sod,
In Flanders Fields.

No lark is nigh:
Aloft, a plane (man's eagle of the sky)
Is strewing wreaths on those who lie
In Flanders Fields.

No resting soul need wake to weep
For faith mistrusted to our keep:
His heritage is peaceful sleep—
In Flanders Fields.

IN OLE KINTUCKY

Dey greets you wid a nod an' smile,
    Way down in Ole Kintucky,
Dat maiks you feel lak life's wuth w'ile
    Way down in Ole Kintucky:
Dar's honey floatin' on de breeze,
Dar's coolin' shade beneaf de trees,
An' gurls ez purtty ez you please,
    Way down in Ole Kintucky.

Dey duzen stan' yore sass an' slack,
    Way down in Ole Kintucky,
Ef you hit dem dey hits you back,
    Way down in Ole Kintucky:
Dar's mountains an' dar's rollin' hills,
Dar's gullies, bab'lin' brooks an' rills,
An' dar's sum hiddin coppah stills
    Way down in Ole Kintucky.

Dar's cole, dar's ine, dar's salt an' oil,
    Way down in Ole Kintucky;
An' lebel fiel's ob fertile soil,
    Way down in Ole Kintucky:
Dey raises backah, co'n an' rye,
Dey ages lickah, bye de bye,
To wet yore whistle w'en youse dry,
    Way down in Ole Kintucky.

Dar's Colonels an' dar's Majahs, bofe,
　Way down in Ole Kintucky,
Dat doan do nothin' 'ceptin loaf,
　Way down in Ole Kintucky:
Dar's famus grass, long, sof' an' blue,
Dar's thairbred runnahs, trottahs, too:
An' dar's a welcome waitin' you,
　Way down in Ole Kintucky.

FACTS

Triumphant Sable Heroes homeward turning,
Arrayed in medals, bright, and half-healed scars,
Has service, life, and limb been given earning
Trophies, issued at the hand of Mars?

If your sole gain has been these "marks of battle,"
If valient deeds insure no greater claim,
If you are still to be the herder's cattle,
Then ill spilt blood fell short of Freedom's aim.

Democracy means more than empty letters,
And Liberty far more than partly free;
Yet, both are void as long as men, in fetters,
Are at eclipse with Opportunity.

A GRAY DAY

The skies are hung with sullen clouds,
A fine mist chills the air,
And earth is wrapt in heavy shrouds
Of stillness and despair.

The birds that sang, so merrily,
Deserters are to-day;
Once laughing brooks sigh mournfully
'Neath skies of leaden gray.

ETERNITY

Vast realm beyond the gate of death,
Where craven scavengers and kings,
Alike, with passing final breath,
Relinquish claim to earthly things.

Endless, unexplored expanse,
Where souls, bereft of mortal clay,
Wander at will, in peace, perchance—
Perchance in strife, who dare would say?

IN STRIPES

Two rail pert sma't ellicks, fresh
      frum Smif's Normal School,
Figgahed dey maik sport ob me,
      played me fo' a fool;
Tuk me to Parkah's Garden, whar
      dey keeps de Bears,
Elephants, an' Tigahs, Lines an'
      Billjen Hares.

We seen a Hipinpotomus, we seen
      a tall Giraff,
An' heaps ob ringtail monkies
      an' Hyenahs dat laff:
Den nex' we spied a critah
      astan' in' 'mouchin' hay,
De boys called him a Zebra
      frum doun in Africay.

Den dey side glanced each uddah,
      thot dey had me right,
"Cast dair fly" fo' suckahs an'
      etspected me to bite.
But 'ste'd, I looked him obah,
      frum his head to his tail,
An' I seed plain he's jes a
      hoss, doin' time in jail.

GONE WEST

O. W. D.

I often wonder, Oscar,
How it fares with you;
Do you look down and smile on us,
From that vast realm of blue?

Tell me, Brother, do you hear
The belching cannon's roar?
Does their death-dealing thunder break
Your peace on yonder shore?

I seem to hear you answering,
That toil and pain and woe
And care and strife—ah! yes, and death
Were left behind, below.

SUNSET

Round appearing,
Illuminant fire,
Built in space,
Shedding heat,
Traveling westward;
Your photosphere
Conflicts
With dwindl'ing light
Of stricken day,
At dying hour.
Emerging from
The reek appears
At distant edge of earth,
A straightened rainbow
Reaching far into the sky—
You are an artist, Sun!

TRACIN' TALES

No doubt dat you lak to know
     jes whut wuz ailin' us,
Why me and Maffew Pleasen'view
     had dat tremandus fuss;
So I'll just splain, ez bes' I kin,
     how it dun cum erbout,
An' leab de placin' ob de blame
     fo' you to figgah out.

Furst, Maffew sed, Wash Dudley tole
     May Belle Hannah Lee
Sum mighty, mighty ugly tales kincernin'
     Nance an' me.
Den w'en I goes to Dudley
     an' ast him wor it so,
He sed, he only ovah heared Jack
     tellin' Ismah Lowe.

Den I goes straight to Ismah, an'
     Iss sen's me to Jack,
An' Jack sed his wife got it frum
     Ann Marildah Black;
Right on to Ann Marildah's
     I ambles on mah way,
To fine dat she had bin enformed
     by Belledonah Grey.

Boun' dat I'd hab de truf fo' long,
   I tuk out once mo';
An' soon Ise stan'in', hat in han',
   et Belledonah's do';
An' w'en I broached her 'bout it, she sed,
   ob co'se 'twas true,
Caze it cum confidensul frum
   Maffew Pleasen'view.

A DISAGREEMENT

You say "That man was made to mourn."
Would you have me believe it—
Believe earth holds no recompense
Until death bids me leave it—
Believe there is but misery
And toil on toil, in store for me?

No. I do not, cannot believe,
While heaven smiles above me,
That I was doom'd on earth to mourn
With naught to. cheer or love me.
Wise Bard, although your dirge rings true,
I do not agree with you.

EVERYWHERE

How dare you question Him, or doubt,
With proof conclusive all about?
What basis has your faith and hope
If grave and death conclude your scope?
Do you not see, as here you stand,
The working of His Master Hand?
Behold you not in field and stream
Presence of His power, supreme?
He is a solace to the poor
In purse and spirit; He is more.
An all-wise Counsel to the meek;
A place of refuge for the weak;
His Omnipresence fills the air!
Behold Him, doubter, everywhere!

SINGIN' AN' PRAYIN'

De hardes' ob hard rows we hoes
Fo' little pay, de goo' Lawd knows.
Yet we hab kep' de heart to sing
Enspite ob dat ah sort ob t'ing.
Aldough de outlook ain't so bright
An' t'ings doan seem to go jes right,
We still is mighty glad to say
Dat we ain't plum fo'got to pray.

RAIN

The clouds are shedding tears of joy,
They fall with rhythmic beat
Upon the earth, and soon destroy
Dust dunes and waves of heat.

Each falling drop enforcement bears
To river, lake and rill,
And sweet refreshment gladly shares
With wooded dell and hill.

Every flower, bud and leaf,
Each blossom, branch and tree
Distills the rain, 'tis my belief,
To feed the honey bee.

I pity every wretch I find
Who, frowning in disdain,
Is deaf and dumb and also blind
To beauty in the rain.

THE NARCISSUS

Seemingly dead, bent, brown and dried,
Unnoticed on yon shelf, she lay;
Until a voice within her cried,
"Awake! 'tis Ressurrection Day."

A slender blade of palest green
From her inner soul crept out,
Timid, fearful to be seen,
A lone adventurer—in doubt.

Then bolder shoots of deeper hue
Sprang resolutely into view:
And, centered in their midst, appeared
A stem whose head was ever reared
Upward toward the sun and light,
Until at last, in raiment white,
A flower, full blown upon the breeze,
Did freely waft perfume to please—
You and me.

MAH DEPEN'ABLE FREN'

He doan care how po' I am,
Or dat folks calls me "Luckless Sam,"
Or dat Ise black, 'sted white or red,
Ez long ez I pat his ole head,
An' let him scratch his fuzz an' fleas
Erbout de place whar ebb he please.

He's bin wid me thoo thick an' thin;
Stood by mah side w'en mah blood kin
Done turnt me loose to sink or swim,
An' let me tell mah woes to him;
Jes laid his ole head on mah knee
An' good ez sed, depen' on me.

Las' Toosday mo'nin', jes 'bout ten,
Dog body-snatchers cot mah fren'
An' put him in de dog lock up,
Long side en onree, mangy pup;
An' dar he lay, paws cross his face,
Ershame to be in sech a place.

Aldough it tuk mah pile, ni' bout,
Doun' I wen' an' bailed him out;
An' dat ole boy jes understood
Ez good ez enybody c'u'd;
Kaze w'en he seen me makin' bail
He 'gan to bark an' wag his tail.

Den, I paid mah las' 'hole dollah
Fo' dem license on his collah,
Fust class, gent'man dog's permit
To let him go whar he sees fit,
Thout bein' pestard by de scamps
Dat prey on po' fo' footed tramps.

ONE WORD

If I had mighty wings to fly,
I d soar aloft in youder sky,
And paint with fire, to never die,
One word—Mother!

Then far out on the desert waste,
In glist'ning sands again I'd trace,
So deep that naught could e'er erase,
One word—Mother!

DE DRUM MAJAH

He's struttin' sho ernuff,
Wearin' a lady's muff
En' ways erpon his head,
Red coat ob reddest red,
Purtty white satin ves',
Gole braid ercross de ches';
Goo'ness! he cuts a stunt,
Prancin' out dar in frunt,
    Leadin' his ban'.

W'en dat ah whistle blows,
Each man behine him knows
'Zacklee whut he mus' do;
You bet! he dues it, too.
W'en dat brass stick he twirls,
Ole maids an' lub-sick gurls
Looks on wid longin' eyes,
Dey simpley idolize
    Dat han'sum man.

Sweet fife an' piccalo,
Bofe warblin' sof' an' lo',
Slide ho'n an' saxophones,
Jazz syncopated tones,
Snare drum an' lead cornet,
Alto an' clarinet,
Las', but not least, dar cum
Cymbals an' big bass drum—
    O! whut a ban'!

Cose, we all undahstan'
Each piece he'ps maik de ban',
But dey all mus' be led,
Sum one mus' be de head:
No doubt, de centipede
Has all de laigs he need,
But take erway de head,
Po' centipede am dead;
    So am de ban'.

PRETTY FLOWER

Truly thou lovest pretty flowers,
For pretty flower, thyself, thou art.
May I, if tenderly I pluck thee,
Make fast thy tendrils to my heart—
    Pretty Flower?

And should Fate deem thee answer, pluck me!
Would one of meager courage dare
To place the hand he feels unworthy
Upon a spotless lily, fair,
    Pretty Flower?

PURCAUTION

Dey think I is "set" an' "fo'gee,"
An' dey lub to sneer an' laff,
Caze I duzen fancy black cats
Crossin' cross mah moon-lit paf.
An' dey calls me "supahstitious,
Ignant, emptee headed fool,
Relick ob days, dead an' buried
Befo' man invented school."

Dey doan stop w'en black cats cross 'em;
Aftah sun down, sweeps de flo';
Cum in yore house thoo de parlah;
Go out by de kitchen do';
Hang dair hats erpon de bed-stead;
Sweep dair feets off wid de broom;
Two will sit deysef on one chair,
Dats p'ovidin' dar is room.

Dey doan feah "thirteen" nor "Friday";
Dey puts on de lef' shoe furst;
Lubs to do whut am fo'biddin',
Jes to aggravate de wurst.
Dey duz dair way; I duz mah way;
Many folks hab many mines;
I jes ain't de sort, I reckon,
To defi de bad luck signs.

MY GRIEVANCE

Yes, I admit a grievance.
I also boldly challenge you—
Come stand where I once stood and fell!
I dare say you will do as well.

Yes, I have long been underpaid,
Although my brain and brawn has made
You rich. O! when do I commence
Receiving honest recompense?

Yes, I am lynched. Is it that I
Must without judge or jury die?
Though innocent, am I accursed
To quench the mob's blood-thirsty thirst?

Yes, I am mocked. Pray tell me why!
Did not my brothers freely die
For you, and your Democracy—
That each and all alike be free?

Yes, I am loyal. But how long
Must I subsist on bitter wrong?
How long shall I give smile for blow,
How long! How long! I ask to know?

Yes, I admit a grievance.
I also boldly challenge you—
Come stand where I once stood and fell!
I dare say you will do as well.

KASSEL B'ILDIN'

Hab you evah laid 'wake dreamin'
B'ildin' kassels in de air,
Wid de windahs purtty stain glass,
Marbell hall, and windin' stair;
An' a drive ob snow white pebbells
Runnin' plum up to de stabell,
Cross a lawn, dats green an' lebell
Ez a bran new bilyard tabell?

Ise dun dun dat varie thin', Sah!
An' I wondah kin dar be
Eny uddah foolish creachah
Kassel b'ildin', jes lak me.
But it doan hu't none, I figgah,
An' I fines it mighty fine,
Jes alayin' b'ildin' kassels,
W'en dar's nuthin' on mah mine.

UNFLINCHINGLY

When tabes claims my useless frame,
And I am with my fathers laid,
I want it said that when he came,
I met him—met him unafraid.

Unflinchingly, full-trustingly,
I hope to face his icy breath,
And step into Eternity
To comfort, through the gate of death.

TOUSSAINT L'OUVERTURE

Through ages down Time's ceaseless span,
An endless, vivid caravan,
His mem'ry wends to ever be
An inspiration to the Free.

Fearless, black, unlettered slave,
From nowhere, sprang in time to save
The freedom of a fault'ring band,
A tremble 'neath a tyrant's hand.

Tricked, trapped, ah, yes, betrayed!
He died a man's death, unafraid;
And dying thus gave proof that he
Was fit to live—eternally.

MASQUERADING

The lips so often frame a smile
While the eyes in salt tears swim:
And heart, repellent cup of bile,
Is filled to kiss the brim.

Oft firm and stern we find a face,
Devoid of outward sign,
A mask before the dwelling place
Of happiness divine.

SANDY

Its bin ni ontoe three years
Since mah Goo' Man, Sandy,
Marched erway, twixt sighs an' tears,
Frum his own Mirandy.
Out yondah on de battle fiel',
Whar de bustin' bullits squeal,
An you offen miss a meal,
Wuz mah Goo' Man, Sandy.

Now de smoke am cleahed erway,
An' mah Goo' Man, Sandy,
Is cumin' home dis verah day—
Home to his Mirandy.
Cumin' bac' to co'n fiel's green,
Wid de snap-beans growin' tween,
To de chile he's nevah seen,
An' to his Mirandy.